suffering & evil

Scott Petty

Little Black Books: Suffering and Evil
© Matthias Media 2010

Matthias Media
(St Matthias Press Ltd ACN 067 558 365)
PO Box 225
Kingsford NSW 2032
Australia
Telephone: (02) 9663 1478; international: +61-2-9663-1478
Facsimile: (02) 9663 3265; international: +61-2-9663-3265
Email: info@matthiasmedia.com.au
Internet: www.matthiasmedia.com.au

Matthias Media (USA)
Telephone: 724 964 8152; international: +1-724-964-8152
Facsimile: 724 964 8166; international: +1-724-964-8166
Email: sales@matthiasmedia.com
Internet: www.matthiasmedia.com

ISBN 978 1 921441 76 9

Cover design and typesetting by Matthias Media.

Contents

Introduction

There's one topic that virtually every Christian has questions about, and that's the topic of suffering and evil. It's a massive topic that needs to be handled with precision and compassion. This is because suffering and evil affect people in horrible ways, and when someone suffers horribly they often want to know why. We want to give people answers that are true, but we also want to be sensitive to their pain. But it is not always easy to give precise and sensitive answers when people are suffering.

Part of the problem in answering these questions with precision and compassion is that we cannot see God with our eyes or talk to him face to face when we're suffering.

Let me explain. Even though I generally don't trust politicians, I reckon that if the leader of our country came over to my place for afternoon tea, it would help. Maybe if we kicked a soccer ball around in the backyard I could tell him what was on my mind. I could say something like, "I'm a bit worried about the state of the economy and deteriorating public services like healthcare. Nice kick, by the way."

And then he might say, "I'm going to look at those two issues this coming week, so I'll get back to you".

And then I might remember that I got a speeding ticket last Saturday. And I could say to him, "Um, also, I got a speeding ticket last Saturday, and I think it's a bit unfair. Can you get me out of it?"

And after he dived to stop my attempt on goal, he might say, "Last Saturday? Consider it done, Scott." And as he left my place to go play soccer next door he might turn to me and say, "Thanks for having me around. We'll be in touch."

I really think it would be easier to trust the leader of the country if I could see him face to face and talk things through with him. It's not that I don't believe he exists, but a personal appearance would help me to have faith in what he's doing when things look a little crook. I reckon it's a bit like that with God when you are suffering or afflicted by evil. It's difficult to trust all that he's doing when we don't get to see him face to face.

The other part of the problem is that it is difficult to work out everything that's going on when we can't see the whole picture. Our perspective of evil and suffering is limited, small as we are. Suffering can seem so pointless from our human perspective.

Some people ask about suffering because of their own intense suffering; others ask from a more abstract, intellectual curiosity about why so much suffering exists in the world. Either way, the question of suffering is a pressing one.

Suffering is real

The very first thing the book of Job teaches us about suffering is that it is real. It is a real part of life, even for followers of God, and even though they are promised all the riches of eternal life.

Job's story is a pretty grim one: he suffers intensely and without explanation. He doesn't know what has gone on in the heavenly council. He doesn't know that God has accepted a deal with Satan to test Job and see if he will stay true to God and continue to fear him. Imagine being Job: within the space of a few minutes, the world he had built around him was shattered. This blameless and upright man lost all his wealth and his sons and daughters, and then experienced debilitating physical illness, all at the hands of Satan. His suffering was so intense that when his friends came to see him they could barely recognize him.

Job's suffering was real. It wasn't imagined. So the first thing we need to understand about suffering is that it is part of the Christian

However, there is a book in the Bible that pulls back the curtain to give us a glimpse of the heavenly perspective on evil and suffering and related questions. It's called 'Job'. Job is an ancient and much-loved yet often misunderstood part of the Old Testament. It makes a massive contribution to this topic so we will look closely at what Job teaches us about God and faith, particularly with respect to evil and suffering.

If you don't know the story of Job then you should put this book down now, open your Bible to the book of Job and read the first two chapters. Go on, do it.

To summarize: Job was a righteous and blessed guy. He was the greatest man in the East in terms of his wealth—7,000 sheep, 3,000 camels, 500 pairs of oxen, 500 donkeys—because in those days you measured wealth in terms of livestock, not BMWs, flat screens or holiday houses. With seven sons and three daughters he had the complete family. But he was also the greatest man in the East in terms of his morality (he was upright and blameless), his wisdom (he feared God and shunned evil) and his spirituality (he offered sacrifices on behalf of his children just in case they cursed God in their hearts when they'd had a couple of lazy beers at their barbeques). Satan (whose name, by the way, means the 'accuser') accused Job of fearing God only because he was so blessed by God. Satan challenged God to strike Job and take away everything he had, to see if Job really feared God or was only into God as long as he profited nicely out of it. When Job proved faithful after the first round of suffering—the destruction of his livestock, servants and children—Satan had another crack at Job, this time inflicting painful sores all over Job's body. By the end of the second chapter Job is sitting in the dust, scraping the pus out of his wounds with a piece of broken coffee cup, and wishing that his wife would shut up.

In a nutshell, that is the opening scene in the story of Job. In the chapters that follow we'll also look at what the New Testament contributes to the topic of evil and suffering, but we will spend most of our time with Job. We can learn a lot by listening in on this ancient wise guy.

CHAPTER 1

The question of suffering

Have you suffered recently? Are you suffering right now? Do y
expect to experience suffering soon? Probably not. Nobody exp
it—that's part of what makes it so bad.

Perhaps you have very little personal experience of suf
Every now and again my son James feels like he suffers
injustice. Usually it's just because we've taken a toy from
he has snatched off his younger brother. But he puts his
his eyes and lays his whole body prone on the grour
of silent and inconsolable grief. Obviously, he doesr
experience of real suffering.

On the other hand, the topic of suffering r
personal for you. You may have had an intensely r
of disease or death, rape or abortion, disappoint
divorce or broken relationships. You might kr
of repeated failure and loneliness.

life. We are not always good at recognizing this; we love to think that we've got it all together, and we tend to deny that problems exist.

Take, for example, the Russian ex-president Vladimir Putin. I really like Vladimir Putin because he's a macho, man's man kind of guy—not at all like most politicians, who look like they should eat more red meat and get a sun tan. Putin pumps iron and goes hunting. He's kind of what Arnold Schwarzenegger would be like if he was a politician. Wait a minute … Anyway, during an important diplomatic conference in Russia while Putin was president, he used a luxury German travel bus (complete with all the bells and whistles) to take the presidents and prime ministers from important countries on a sightseeing tour of Moscow. Now, Moscow is notorious for its crime, especially mafia-related organized crime. But Putin continually denied that such crime existed in his capital city—until it became obvious to everyone on the trip that his 'luxury German travel bus' had in fact been stolen from Belarus or the Ukraine (or somewhere like that) and sold using false documents. Putin was in denial.

Here's another example: in 2004, teen stars Ashley and Mary-Kate Olsen addressed rumours of a cocaine addiction and an eating disorder. "Being in the public eye," Ashley told *People Magazine*, "you're labelled that you have an eating disorder … We don't have problems! There's nothing to worry about …" "If I had an addiction," Mary-Kate added, "I would be in a thingy—like Promises, the Malibu [rehab] place. You don't see me there. So, like, come on. It's crazy."[1] But only two months afterwards, *the same magazine* reported that Mary-Kate's father had checked her in to an exclusive clinic in Utah, known for its scenic mountain views and its intensive approach to treating eating disorders and drug addictions. Mary-Kate was in denial. So was McDonald's, because as soon as Mary-Kate left the clinic she joined her sister Ashley as a spokesperson for their Happy Meals. Apparently drug addiction and eating disorders are just what you need when you're promoting family restaurants and Happy Meals! That's denial. In our society we are masters at denying our problems.

But Job does not deny there's a problem; he doesn't deny his suffering. You see it in chapters 1 and 2 when he tears his clothes, shaves his head and sits down in the ashes (all signs of intense grief). You also hear it in his words starting at chapter 3:

life. We are not always good at recognizing this; we love to think that we've got it all together, and we tend to deny that problems exist.

Take, for example, the Russian ex-president Vladimir Putin. I really like Vladimir Putin because he's a macho, man's man kind of guy—not at all like most politicians, who look like they should eat more red meat and get a sun tan. Putin pumps iron and goes hunting. He's kind of what Arnold Schwarzenegger would be like if he was a politician. Wait a minute … Anyway, during an important diplomatic conference in Russia while Putin was president, he used a luxury German travel bus (complete with all the bells and whistles) to take the presidents and prime ministers from important countries on a sightseeing tour of Moscow. Now, Moscow is notorious for its crime, especially mafia-related organized crime. But Putin continually denied that such crime existed in his capital city—until it became obvious to everyone on the trip that his 'luxury German travel bus' had in fact been stolen from Belarus or the Ukraine (or somewhere like that) and sold using false documents. Putin was in denial.

Here's another example: in 2004, teen stars Ashley and Mary-Kate Olsen addressed rumours of a cocaine addiction and an eating disorder. "Being in the public eye," Ashley told *People Magazine*, "you're labelled that you have an eating disorder ... We don't have problems! There's nothing to worry about ..." "If I had an addiction," Mary-Kate added, "I would be in a thingy—like Promises, the Malibu [rehab] place. You don't see me there. So, like, come on. It's crazy."[1] But only two months afterwards, *the same magazine* reported that Mary-Kate's father had checked her in to an exclusive clinic in Utah, known for its scenic mountain views and its intensive approach to treating eating disorders and drug addictions. Mary-Kate was in denial. So was McDonald's, because as soon as Mary-Kate left the clinic she joined her sister Ashley as a spokesperson for their Happy Meals. Apparently drug addiction and eating disorders are just what you need when you're promoting family restaurants and Happy Meals! That's denial. In our society we are masters at denying our problems.

But Job does not deny there's a problem; he doesn't deny his suffering. You see it in chapters 1 and 2 when he tears his clothes, shaves his head and sits down in the ashes (all signs of intense grief). You also hear it in his words starting at chapter 3:

However, there is a book in the Bible that pulls back the curtain to give us a glimpse of the heavenly perspective on evil and suffering and related questions. It's called 'Job'. Job is an ancient and much-loved yet often misunderstood part of the Old Testament. It makes a massive contribution to this topic so we will look closely at what Job teaches us about God and faith, particularly with respect to evil and suffering.

If you don't know the story of Job then you should put this book down now, open your Bible to the book of Job and read the first two chapters. Go on, do it.

To summarize: Job was a righteous and blessed guy. He was the greatest man in the East in terms of his wealth—7,000 sheep, 3,000 camels, 500 pairs of oxen, 500 donkeys—because in those days you measured wealth in terms of livestock, not BMWs, flat screens or holiday houses. With seven sons and three daughters he had the complete family. But he was also the greatest man in the East in terms of his morality (he was upright and blameless), his wisdom (he feared God and shunned evil) and his spirituality (he offered sacrifices on behalf of his children just in case they cursed God in their hearts when they'd had a couple of lazy beers at their barbeques). Satan (whose name, by the way, means the 'accuser') accused Job of fearing God only because he was so blessed by God. Satan challenged God to strike Job and take away everything he had, to see if Job really feared God or was only into God as long as he profited nicely out of it. When Job proved faithful after the first round of suffering—the destruction of his livestock, servants and children—Satan had another crack at Job, this time inflicting painful sores all over Job's body. By the end of the second chapter Job is sitting in the dust, scraping the pus out of his wounds with a piece of broken coffee cup, and wishing that his wife would shut up.

In a nutshell, that is the opening scene in the story of Job. In the chapters that follow we'll also look at what the New Testament contributes to the topic of evil and suffering, but we will spend most of our time with Job. We can learn a lot by listening in on this ancient wise guy.

CHAPTER 1

The question of suffering

Have you suffered recently? Are you suffering right now? Do you expect to experience suffering soon? Probably not. Nobody expects it—that's part of what makes it so bad.

Perhaps you have very little personal experience of suffering. Every now and again my son James feels like he suffers a great injustice. Usually it's just because we've taken a toy from him that he has snatched off his younger brother. But he puts his hands over his eyes and lays his whole body prone on the ground in an act of silent and inconsolable grief. Obviously, he doesn't have much experience of real suffering.

On the other hand, the topic of suffering might be deeply personal for you. You may have had an intensely painful experience of disease or death, rape or abortion, disappointment or depression, divorce or broken relationships. You might know the private pain of repeated failure and loneliness.

Some people ask about suffering because of their own intense suffering; others ask from a more abstract, intellectual curiosity about why so much suffering exists in the world. Either way, the question of suffering is a pressing one.

Suffering is real

The very first thing the book of Job teaches us about suffering is that it is real. It is a real part of life, even for followers of God, and even though they are promised all the riches of eternal life.

Job's story is a pretty grim one: he suffers intensely and without explanation. He doesn't know what has gone on in the heavenly council. He doesn't know that God has accepted a deal with Satan to test Job and see if he will stay true to God and continue to fear him. Imagine being Job: within the space of a few minutes, the world he had built around him was shattered. This blameless and upright man lost all his wealth and his sons and daughters, and then experienced debilitating physical illness, all at the hands of Satan. His suffering was so intense that when his friends came to visit him they could barely recognize him.

Job's suffering was real. It wasn't imagined. So the first thing we need to understand about suffering is that it is part of the Christian

… Job opened his mouth and cursed the day of his birth. He said:

"May the day of my birth perish,
    and the night it was said, 'A boy is born!'
That day—may it turn to darkness;
    may God above not care about it;
    may no light shine upon it." (vv. 1-4)

And in verses 24-26:

"For sighing comes to me instead of food;
    my groans pour out like water.
What I feared has come upon me;
    what I dreaded has happened to me.
I have no peace, no quietness;
    I have no rest, but only turmoil."

Job's suffering is very real. It affects every aspect of his life: his wealth, his family, his standing in society, and his physical and mental health. There is no point denying it, neither for Job nor for us. We live in a world in which people suffer, and sometimes unjustly. When that happens to you like it happened to Job, then frankly it is better to gasp in despair, or to confess your loss of hope or sense of frustration, than to pretend everything is OK. God will not blame you for that kind of honesty.

Suffering is not God's punishment for your sin

As well as teaching us that suffering is real, Job teaches us much more important things about suffering. One is that suffering is not necessarily God's punishment for your sin. If you suffer, that is not God's coded way of saying that you have been a naughty boy or girl.

In February 2009, the worst bushfires ever to sweep the Australian state of Victoria killed 173 people and destroyed 2,000 homes. A Pentecostal pastor told the media that the fires were God's judgement on Victoria for passing laws that permitted doctors to perform abortions legally. He was saying that Victoria burned because it had passed sinful legislation. He was making a direct connection between sin and suffering.

But we simply can't make that direct connection. Suffering may not be linked to specific sin at all. We can see clear evidence of this in Job's life. He is described in Job 1:1 as "blameless and upright" and a man who "feared God and shunned evil". He takes seriously not just his own sin, but also the potential sins of his family. And

even though he is struck with awful calamity, he does not sin by cursing God. Despite his righteousness throughout chapter 1, he is struck with painful sores all over his body in chapter 2—so painful, in fact, that the relief of scraping his sores with broken pottery was worth any added injury it caused him. Just to make things even harder, his wife begs him to curse God and die so that his suffering will end. And still Job refuses to sin in what he says about God. Make no mistake: sometimes people suffer unjustly. Suffering is not necessarily God's punishment for sin. Though Job's suffering is unfathomable, nowhere in the book of Job does the author of the book (or even God) record any sin of Job. Job is presented throughout as righteous.

Three of Job's friends come to comfort him, but as they come close they barely recognize him because his suffering is so severe. And so they sit with him for seven days in silence, which is about the most useful thing they end up doing for Job. But when the silence is broken, Job's friends start saying that his suffering is because of his personal sinfulness. For example, Eliphaz says in chapter 4:

> "Consider now: Who, being innocent, has ever perished?
>> Where were the upright ever destroyed?
> As I have observed, those who plough evil
>> and those who sow trouble reap it." (vv. 7-8)

In other words: "Job, your suffering shows us that you are not innocent; you have done evil so now you are suffering evil". And it sounds simple, doesn't it? You do good, good comes back to you; you play with fire, you get burned. What goes around, comes around. That's the 'instant karma' view of life, which has its origins in Hinduism and Buddhism. The formula is simple: you do good, you get rewarded directly; you do evil, you get punished directly. But we can see that suffering is *not* necessarily God's punishment for specific sin by the way God reacts to what Job's friends have said. When God eventually breaks his silence, he says that he is angry with Job's friends (Job 42:7) and their simplistic little formula. They did not say the right things about God.

Sometimes people *do* suffer directly on account of their sin. If I got drunk and then got in my car and caused an accident, it would be fair enough if I lost my job and went to jail. But we cannot say that suffering is simplistically and mathematically always the result of a particular sin. The book of Job does not let us do that. Neither does Jesus. In John 9, Jesus is about to heal a man who was born blind. The disciples ask Jesus who sinned—the man himself or his parents—to cause him to be born blind. Jesus tells them that the man was blind not on account of his sin or his parents' sin, but so that God might showcase his work in the blind man's life when he was healed from his blindness.[2]

Why do we suffer?

So if Job's suffering is not linked with his sin, what is it linked to? What causes it?

In Romans 8, the Apostle Paul tells us that the whole creation is groaning under the weight of sin and judgement—so that's partly the answer. This world is a place of suffering because mankind brought sin into the world. Nothing is all that it should be. The sinfulness that we inherited from our first parents, Adam and Eve, is partly what lies behind Job's suffering. Even a casual observer can see that human evil causes some of the suffering in Job's life and in our lives. But behind human evil is Satan, the one who is always accusing and trying to deceive the people of God. And behind Satan stands God, who is purposely restraining Satan (although not fully restraining evil) in our world.

There's more to say about evil in the next chapter, but for now it is enough to say that life is not as simple as 'You get rewarded if you do good and you suffer immediately if you do bad'.

For now, let's also try to get a hold on what God is doing with our suffering. Part of what he is doing is drawing us close to him. CS Lewis said that pain is God's megaphone to rouse a deaf world.[3] Suffering reminds us that the playthings we fill our lives with are just playthings and not the important things. When we suffer we have cause to cast ourselves upon the mercy and goodness of God. You may never be able to make sense of it, but you can draw closer to God through it. You may never know what other good comes from your suffering; you may never find out. Job never found out that his own faithfulness under suffering justified God in front of Satan and all the angels. And yet Job's suffering drew him into a closer relationship with, and understanding of, God. If you have ever read the whole book, you will know that Job cries out incessantly in search of an audience with God. When God eventually breaks his silence, he takes Job's breath away and blows his mind, and at the end of the book Job trusts God more than he does at the start.

I also reckon that the man at the end of the book of Job is even more righteous, more Jesus-like, than he was at the start of the book. In the very last chapter, there's this beautiful picture of God making Job more prosperous in the latter part of his life than in the first. Job offered sacrifices for the friends he argued with for 35 chapters. All his old mates came around to give him consolation and presents. God gave him seven more sons and three more daughters. They were the most beautiful women in the land. Job gave them names that sounded like sweet spices and, contrary to the convention of the day, he also gave them shares in the family wealth along with their brothers.

I just reckon that we're supposed to see in this beautiful picture not so much that Job is luckier than he used to be, but that he's a better man than he used to be; a better man than he would have been if he had not suffered in the first place. (Funny—this is exactly what the Apostle Paul said in Romans 8:28-29 when he said that God works everything—*all* things—for the good of those who love him, to make them become more like Jesus.) That could not have happened if Job had not suffered.

Who can understand why people suffer unjustly sometimes? And yet there are some things in life under God that we can learn in no other way than by suffering. That is why it was so right for

Job to cry out, but it would have been so wrong for him to charge God with wrongdoing.

The remarkable thing is that what happened to Job back then happens to people today, more often than you might think. I know families who have had children die in childbirth. I know families who have had children born with vital organs severely debilitated and even missing. I know people whose kids have gone off the rails to live a drug-addicted life on the streets. I know people whose husbands and wives have turned away from Jesus and who now taunt them because of their faith. I know people whose husbands and wives have suffered illnesses to the point where they no longer even recognize or acknowledge the person they have been married to for decades.

Each of these people who have suffered (and who in many cases continue to suffer) are righteous people who love Jesus, love their neighbours, and are pillars of their local churches. What do you think they did when they discovered their sad news? Did they curse God to his face? Charge God with wrongdoing? Curse God and die? No. Remarkably, like Job, through their pain they recognized that bad things sometimes happen, even to Christians. They drew closer to God and became more like Jesus. It has not been easy for any of them, but it has been possible for all of them.

When you suffer unjustly, you can push God away or you can draw closer to him. You can let suffering make you a bitter Christian or a better Christian. When you suffer there will sometimes be mystery; the question is whether there will also be faith. Faith says, "The LORD gave and the LORD has taken away; may the name of the LORD be praised" (Job 1:21), even when there is mystery in suffering. Faith says, "Shall we accept good from God, and not trouble?" (Job 2:10), precisely at the moment when we are in trouble.

God knows what it is like to suffer

The last thing to say here is that God knows what it's like to be without sin and yet suffer loss. There are a few points of stark connection between Jesus and Job: both are blameless and upright; both fear God and shun evil; and both offer up sacrifices for the sins of others. Do you think that Job's pain is lost on God? Surely not, for God knew even before he made the world that he would offer up his own Son to death for the sake of others—sinners like you and me. Before Job was ever dreamt up by his parents, God had predestined losing his most precious one, the Lord Jesus, on the cross. Have you ever thought about the innocent blood shed by Christ? Have you ever considered that his tears and the tears of his heavenly father were shed not because of their own evil, but because it was the only way of dealing with our evil?

You are not alone in your unjust suffering. Job is not alone in his unjust suffering. Even God knows what it is like to suffer because of the sins of others. When we look at the cross in the midst of our suffering, the one conclusion we cannot come to is that God doesn't care. He has suffered much more than you and me.

. Despite what the dreamers think, the problem of evil
solved by all of us just learning to love each other a little
il is real. Tax cuts, early warning systems, rock'n'roll …
hese will eliminate it.

could—and will—one day eliminate evil; but of course
mean that he will eliminate all evildoers and sinners as
e process, which doesn't really help anyone who doesn't
. He's actually holding off to give people the opportunity
nd trust in him (2 Pet 3:7-10).

the meantime we need to get used to evil as an intrinsic
e world we know, not an interruption to reality. It is part
l of human existence, as Job recognizes clearly in Job 16:

open their mouths to jeer at me;
y strike my cheek in scorn
l unite together against me.
as turned me over to evil men
l thrown me into the clutches of the wicked." (vv. 10-11)

hand is involved in evil

ortant to see that Satan initiates and brings evil into Job's
campers before the throne of God to make his accusations:

CHAPTER 2

The question of evil

There is a basic question that you face in life if you believe in God: if God is loving *and* powerful, why is there evil in the world? If he is loving, he wouldn't want evil to exist; if he is powerful, he doesn't have to put up with it. So why is there evil? Either God is loving but powerless, or he is powerful but nasty—or he doesn't exist at all.

If you don't believe in God, then you don't have to deal with this question. You can just milk the most out of life, even at the expense of others, until you become food for worms when you die. That is the alternative that makes the most sense. But it's not a great alternative, especially for those who cannot milk much out of life because they're born in a poor country or into a disadvantaged family or whatever.

So what do you do with the presence of evil in the world? I am a big fan of iPod technology, especially the iPod nano, because it is just so teeny weeny. It really appeals to my slightly obsessive-compulsive personality. I love how you can put all your music onto it, plus your digital photos as well as some movies. And I really love the way you can sort your songs by playlist, artist, album, genre, whatever. I can control where things go, everything has its place, everything is neat and tidy. And I can switch it off and put it in my pocket whenever I please.

But when you learn about how God interacts with evil in the world, you realize that God is not an iPod nano. I can't control where everything goes. Everything does not have its place according to my way of thinking. Everything is not neat and tidy. I cannot contain God in my pocket, and I cannot turn him off. There is a wild and mysterious aspect to the way he handles evil that I cannot quite get my head around, even though I know that he is good.

Evil is alive and kicking in the world

The first thing the book of Job teaches us about evil is that it is alive and kicking in the world.

What did you think when you read the start of Job's story, as his oxen and donkeys were carried off, or when a firestorm burnt up his sheep and servants, or when raiders carried off his camels,

or even when a tornado destroyed the hou[se]
in? Were you waiting for things to go back[...]
was afflicted with painful sores all over his[...]
was just a figment of his imagination? Or d[...]
with you?

I think what happened to Job resonates[...]
evil in operation every day. Evil abounds[...]
in Job's world, theft and violence threaten[...]
Perhaps some of us live lives of privilege, i[...]
of what we need, and just about everythin[...]
that tricks us into thinking that we are en[...]
so that when trouble happens in our live[s]
like a commercial break on TV: it's just an[...]
programming. We are mildly annoyed th[at]
has been interrupted, and we expect thin[gs]
quickly. But evil is not an interruption t[o]
kicking.

Despite what our education experts s[...]
solve the problem of evil. The Nazis w[ere]
educated people of their time. Despite wh[...]
the problem of evil will not be solved by a[...]

"Does Job fear God for nothing? Have you not put a hedge around him and his household and everything he has? You have blessed the works of his hands …" (Job 1:9-10). In other words, Job only follows God because he's getting a good deal out of it. The fact that the name 'Satan' actually means 'accuser' tells us what he really does: he accuses and deceives. That is what happened in the garden of Eden: he accused God of withholding good from Adam and Eve, and he deceived them into disobeying God. From the very beginning, Satan's hand has been involved in evil. And that is certainly true in Job's life. Satan urges God to "strike everything [Job] has" and, upon gaining God's permission, Satan scampers off to bring destruction to Job's world. Satan initiates and then causes the devastation in Job's life.

But Satan is restrained by God

Although Satan initiates and causes the tragedy in Job's life, we also need to see that God restrains Satan's activity. I once heard Jerry Seinfeld wonder who aliens would think was in charge if they landed on earth and saw a man taking his dog for a walk. It would look like the dog was in charge, wouldn't it? The dog is always out in front. If the dog wants to sniff around telegraph poles, the man has to wait. The clincher is that if the dog goes to the toilet, it's the man who has to scoop it up and put it in a plastic bag, which he then has to carry around for the rest of the walk. Whenever I walk a dog now, I'm always conscious of alien visitors, so I make sure that I use the leash to control the dog. I use the leash to set the limits of the dog's activity. I will let it go only so far and then no further.

And that is what God does with Satan. He sets the limits of Satan's activity. God determines that Satan may go so far, but does not permit him to go any further. After all, they are not equal and opposite forces. It is undeniably God who is in charge. Look closely at Job 1:12. Satan has accused Job of following God just to gain prosperity and blessing, and he has challenged God to "strike everything [Job] has, and he will surely curse you to your face". Do you notice what God says to Satan? "Very well, then, everything he has is in your hands, but on the man himself do not lay a finger".

God has got Satan on a leash. "You may go this far but no further", says God. And we can see from Job 1:11-12 that the devil cannot exceed those boundaries; he is held back by the restraining hand of God.

In spite of Satan's accusation and despite the misery that is poured out on Job, Job refuses to curse God, and continues to fear him.

In Job 2, Satan must again go before God to obtain his permission to attack Job: "Stretch out your hand and strike his flesh and bones, and he will surely curse you to your face" (v. 5). God says, "Very well, then, he is in your hands; but you must spare his life" (v. 6). Again God sets the limits of his activity, and although Satan afflicts Job with painful sores, he does not go beyond God's instruction to spare his life.

Satan accuses, he deceives, he initiates and brings disaster upon Job. His hand is only inclined towards evil. But God restrains Satan's activity and limits his evil and influence.

God's hand controls evil

God's hand not only restrains evil but also controls it. He controls evil but is not stained by it. Job is so convinced it is God's hand that controls evil that he does not even recognize secondary causes. He speaks only of God as the first or primary cause of evil.

What I mean is that although a wind knocked down the house that killed Job's children, he looks behind that secondary cause to see God as the primary cause. Although it was the Sabean and

Chaldean raiders who stole his livestock, he looks behind those raiders and sees God as the primary cause. In Job's world view it is not Chaldeans, Sabeans or even tornados that caused his suffering. He looks through those secondary causes and sees God controlling his fortune. And although it was Satan who afflicted him with painful sores, Job even looks through Satan and says, "The LORD gave and the LORD has taken away; may the name of the LORD be praised" (Job 1:21). And in 2:10 he says, "Shall we accept good from God, and not trouble?"

And because God's ultimate control of evil is so important in the book of Job, we never even hear of Satan again after chapter 2. The rest of the book concerns the relationship between God and Job.

Although it is right to say that God's hand controls evil (in the sense that evil is not a force that is capable of overpowering God), God is not stained by evil. This might not make sense to us. If God stands behind the evil in Job's life, it seems crazy to us that Job doesn't accuse God of wrongdoing. But he doesn't. And he is commended for precisely that: not charging God with wrongdoing.

We find it difficult to understand how God can be seen to

CHAPTER 2

The question of evil

There is a basic question that you face in life if you believe in God: if God is loving *and* powerful, why is there evil in the world? If he is loving, he wouldn't want evil to exist; if he is powerful, he doesn't have to put up with it. So why is there evil? Either God is loving but powerless, or he is powerful but nasty—or he doesn't exist at all.

If you don't believe in God, then you don't have to deal with this question. You can just milk the most out of life, even at the expense of others, until you become food for worms when you die. That is the alternative that makes the most sense. But it's not a great alternative, especially for those who cannot milk much out of life because they're born in a poor country or into a disadvantaged family or whatever.

So what do you do with the presence of evil in the world? I am a big fan of iPod technology, especially the iPod nano, because it is just so teeny weeny. It really appeals to my slightly obsessive-compulsive personality. I love how you can put all your music onto it, plus your digital photos as well as some movies. And I really love the way you can sort your songs by playlist, artist, album, genre, whatever. I can control where things go, everything has its place, everything is neat and tidy. And I can switch it off and put it in my pocket whenever I please.

But when you learn about how God interacts with evil in the world, you realize that God is not an iPod nano. I can't control where everything goes. Everything does not have its place according to my way of thinking. Everything is not neat and tidy. I cannot contain God in my pocket, and I cannot turn him off. There is a wild and mysterious aspect to the way he handles evil that I cannot quite get my head around, even though I know that he is good.

Evil is alive and kicking in the world

The first thing the book of Job teaches us about evil is that it is alive and kicking in the world.

What did you think when you read the start of Job's story, as his oxen and donkeys were carried off, or when a firestorm burnt up his sheep and servants, or when raiders carried off his camels, or even when a tornado destroyed the house all his children were in? Were you waiting for things to go back to normal? When Job was afflicted with painful sores all over his body, did you think it was just a figment of his imagination? Or did his troubles resonate with you?

I think what happened to Job resonates with us because we see evil in operation every day. Evil abounds in our world. Just like in Job's world, theft and violence threaten people in our society. Perhaps some of us live lives of privilege, in which we have most of what we need, and just about everything we want. And maybe that tricks us into thinking that we are entitled to such blessings, so that when trouble happens in our lives we think of it almost like a commercial break on TV: it's just an interruption to normal programming. We are mildly annoyed that the progress of life has been interrupted, and we expect things to get back on track quickly. But evil is not an interruption to reality. It is alive and kicking.

Despite what our education experts suggest, education won't solve the problem of evil. The Nazis were some of the best-educated people of their time. Despite what the universities teach, the problem of evil will not be solved by a more even distribution of wealth. Despite what the dreamers think, the problem of evil won't be solved by all of us just learning to love each other a little better. Evil is real. Tax cuts, early warning systems, rock'n'roll ... none of these will eliminate it.

God could—and will—one day eliminate evil; but of course that will mean that he will eliminate all evildoers and sinners as part of the process, which doesn't really help anyone who doesn't trust him. He's actually holding off to give people the opportunity to turn and trust in him (2 Pet 3:7-10).

But in the meantime we need to get used to evil as an intrinsic part of the world we know, not an interruption to reality. It is part and parcel of human existence, as Job recognizes clearly in Job 16:

> "Men open their mouths to jeer at me;
> > they strike my cheek in scorn
> > and unite together against me.
> God has turned me over to evil men
> > and thrown me into the clutches of the wicked." (vv. 10-11)

Satan's hand is involved in evil

It is important to see that Satan initiates and brings evil into Job's life. He scampers before the throne of God to make his accusations:

"Does Job fear God for nothing? Have you not put a hedge around him and his household and everything he has? You have blessed the works of his hands …" (Job 1:9-10). In other words, Job only follows God because he's getting a good deal out of it. The fact that the name 'Satan' actually means 'accuser' tells us what he really does: he accuses and deceives. That is what happened in the garden of Eden: he accused God of withholding good from Adam and Eve, and he deceived them into disobeying God. From the very beginning, Satan's hand has been involved in evil. And that is certainly true in Job's life. Satan urges God to "strike everything [Job] has" and, upon gaining God's permission, Satan scampers off to bring destruction to Job's world. Satan initiates and then causes the devastation in Job's life.

But Satan is restrained by God

Although Satan initiates and causes the tragedy in Job's life, we also need to see that God restrains Satan's activity. I once heard Jerry Seinfeld wonder who aliens would think was in charge if they landed on earth and saw a man taking his dog for a walk. It would look like the dog was in charge, wouldn't it? The dog is always out in front. If the dog wants to sniff around telegraph poles, the man has to wait. The clincher is that if the dog goes to the toilet, it's the man who has to scoop it up and put it in a plastic bag, which he then has to carry around for the rest of the walk. Whenever I walk a dog now, I'm always conscious of alien visitors, so I make sure that I use the leash to control the dog. I use the leash to set the limits of the dog's activity. I will let it go only so far and then no further.

And that is what God does with Satan. He sets the limits of Satan's activity. God determines that Satan may go so far, but does not permit him to go any further. After all, they are not equal and opposite forces. It is undeniably God who is in charge. Look closely at Job 1:12. Satan has accused Job of following God just to gain prosperity and blessing, and he has challenged God to "strike everything [Job] has, and he will surely curse you to your face". Do you notice what God says to Satan? "Very well, then, everything he has is in your hands, but on the man himself do not lay a finger".

God has got Satan on a leash. "You may go this far but no further", says God. And we can see from Job 1:11-12 that the devil cannot exceed those boundaries; he is held back by the restraining hand of God.

In spite of Satan's accusation and despite the misery that is poured out on Job, Job refuses to curse God, and continues to fear him.

In Job 2, Satan must again go before God to obtain his permission to attack Job: "Stretch out your hand and strike his flesh and bones, and he will surely curse you to your face" (v. 5). God says, "Very well, then, he is in your hands; but you must spare his life" (v. 6). Again God sets the limits of his activity, and although Satan afflicts Job with painful sores, he does not go beyond God's instruction to spare his life.

Satan accuses, he deceives, he initiates and brings disaster upon Job. His hand is only inclined towards evil. But God restrains Satan's activity and limits his evil and influence.

God's hand controls evil

God's hand not only restrains evil but also controls it. He controls evil but is not stained by it. Job is so convinced it is God's hand that controls evil that he does not even recognize secondary causes. He speaks only of God as the first or primary cause of evil.

What I mean is that although a wind knocked down the house that killed Job's children, he looks behind that secondary cause to see God as the primary cause. Although it was the Sabean and

Chaldean raiders who stole his livestock, he looks behind those raiders and sees God as the primary cause. In Job's world view it is not Chaldeans, Sabeans or even tornados that caused his suffering. He looks through those secondary causes and sees God controlling his fortune. And although it was Satan who afflicted him with painful sores, Job even looks through Satan and says, "The LORD gave and the LORD has taken away; may the name of the LORD be praised" (Job 1:21). And in 2:10 he says, "Shall we accept good from God, and not trouble?"

And because God's ultimate control of evil is so important in the book of Job, we never even hear of Satan again after chapter 2. The rest of the book concerns the relationship between God and Job.

Although it is right to say that God's hand controls evil (in the sense that evil is not a force that is capable of overpowering God), God is not stained by evil. This might not make sense to us. If God stands behind the evil in Job's life, it seems crazy to us that Job doesn't accuse God of wrongdoing. But he doesn't. And he is commended for precisely that: not charging God with wrongdoing.

We find it difficult to understand how God can be seen to

control evil and yet somehow not be stained by evil. But that is not only the consistent testimony of the book of Job; it also remains the united testimony of all of Scripture. In Deuteronomy Moses says, "his works are perfect, and all his ways are just. A faithful God who does no wrong, upright and just is he" (Deut 32:4). Psalm 89 says that, "Righteousness and justice are the foundation of your throne" (v. 14). In the New Testament Jesus says, "Be perfect, therefore, as your heavenly Father is perfect" (Matt 5:48). And James 1 tells us that "God cannot be tempted by evil, nor does he tempt anyone" (Jas 1:13).

Although Job struggles to understand justice in his current situation, the fact that he remains a believer in the goodness and justice of God is clear from the fact that he wrestles for so long—34 chapters—with it. If he had stopped believing he would have shut up in chapter 3, but he continues because of his overwhelming conviction that God is good.

We don't always know how this all works

Although we can say with confidence that God is good, and that he is sovereignly in control of evil, we cannot always know how or why this is possible. And the problem is not with God; it is with our puny ability to understand his ways.

In the book of Job, Job spends most of his time pleading with God to hear his case and show him justice. God eventually breaks his silence in chapters 38-41 by questioning Job exhaustively. Back then, the scariest beast known to man was the leviathan. It might simply be what we would call the crocodile, but most likely it represented the forces of chaos and evil. So, in a time when the leviathan was feared above all else, God asks Job:

> "Can you pull in the leviathan with a fishhook
>> or tie down his tongue with a rope?
> Can you put a cord through his nose
>> or pierce his jaw with a hook?
> Will he keep begging you for mercy?
>> Will he speak to you with gentle words?" …
>
> "If you lay a hand on him,
>> you will remember the struggle and never do it again!" (Job 41:1-3, 8)

God goes on to point out that any hope of subduing the leviathan is false; "the mere sight of him is overpowering. No-one is fierce enough to rouse him" (Job 41:9-10).

I was a big fan of Steve Irwin, 'The Crocodile Hunter'. He was an infectiously positive guy and a complete nutcase (as you would know if you ever watched one of his shows). And although he was a master at feeding a crocodile at close range, he knew he had little hope of controlling one for more than a few moments. A few years ago, in an appearance at a big awards ceremony, Steve Irwin rose to the stage through a trapdoor, holding a giant snake. As he was carrying on in his usual over-the-top Steve Irwin way, he accidentally fell off the stage, dropping the snake as he fell. The snake sailed through the air and landed in the lap of a well-known sports reporter, biting him on the inner thigh. I don't think that was in the script. There was no-one on earth who could match Steve Irwin's ability with dangerous animals. But Steve Irwin couldn't control a snake, let alone subdue a crocodile, let alone control the forces of chaos and evil. Only God can do that.

And that is God's argument in Job 41. If you are not strong enough to control the leviathan, how can you tell God what to do with evil? Only God has the wisdom to know that. I mean, we can hazard some pretty good guesses as to why God doesn't remove evil entirely. If he eliminated all evil then he would need to eliminate evil people who don't trust in him, so perhaps his delay is to give sinners more time to turn to him (as we noted earlier). Or perhaps God is simply letting evil run its course so that we reap the consequences of our own sinful behaviour. But really, there is a whole chunk of God's control over evil that we cannot understand. Our thinking is too limited, our brains too puny.

But if you have any doubts that the way God deals with evil is wise, you need only consider the death of Jesus. In the death of Jesus, God shapes the murderous intentions of men—the Jewish religious leaders and Roman politicians—into the extraordinary salvation of sinners. Now *that* is wise!

And so we need to be a little like Job. We must not charge God with wrongdoing, or blame him for evil. We need to trust him through the mysterious circumstances of our lives. We need to maintain faith in the goodness and justice of God, even when it is not immediately apparent or understandable in the world around us. If you cannot stand against the crocodile, you cannot stand against the God who made it and the God who controls evil. You cannot stand against the one who restrains the activity of the devil. The answer is to stand *with* him in faith instead.

CHAPTER 3

The question of God

I think we sometimes get bored with God. We think we've heard all there is to hear, and frankly it's not interesting any more, and so we get bored with God. Other times we think he's actually pretty bored with us; he is too far away to really care about all the ins and outs of our little lives. And so if he is bored with us, we might as well be bored with him too.

You can tell when people get bored with God: they fill their lives with playthings and pleasures, or they bury themselves in family or work, so that they don't have to give any attention to the spiritual side of life. So you see men on the golf course instead of at church on Sunday mornings. Or people sleep in because the demands of their busy week—demands they pretty much created for themselves—leave them so tired that Sunday is the only day when they can catch up on rest. People get bored with God so they get busy with other things. Personally, I reckon if you are going to ignore God then you're much better off starting your own religion. There's usually a fair bit of money in it.[4]

In truth though, if you are bored with God then it is probably because you don't know him well enough. One of the good things about thinking through the issue of suffering and evil is that we uncover things about God that we might not have known previously. For instance, we have discovered that God controls evil and directs it for his purposes, yet he is somehow untainted by evil.

There are other interesting things we learn about God when we ponder this issue—things that should surprise you (in a good way).

God is not always predictable

One of the main reasons we get bored with God is that we think God is predictable.

I find romantic comedies and action films to be utterly predictable. Romantic comedies are always the same: 1 hour and 22 minutes long, with Tom Hanks and Meg Ryan, or Julia Roberts and Richard Gere, or Matthew McConaughey and a pretty blonde girl, or Matthew McConaughey and Matthew McConaughey (he's very pretty). Boy meets girl. At first there is no attraction; they might even hate each other. Eventually, after approximately 53 minutes have passed, boy and girl are in love. But then something threatens that love—maybe something in the past, maybe a reckless comment, maybe boy takes undue interest in girl's best friend. Anyway, the tension is resolved somewhat unrealistically and they get married in a rich relative's backyard under sunny skies. Utterly predictable.

I don't think God is predictable though. I don't know what you make of the deal that God makes with Satan in Job 1–2, but it seems pretty clear to me that God takes a big risk with Job. Job's outstanding righteousness caught not only the attention of God, who was very proud of Job (repeatedly calling him "my servant"), but also the attention of Satan. As we saw earlier, Satan sees Job's righteous fear of God and accuses Job of fearing God only for what he could get out of it. You would expect God to tell Satan off, to give him an earful, to tell him straight up that Job fears God not because it benefits him, but because it's just what a righteous man does. That's what you'd predict.

But, surprisingly, God puts his whole reputation and his way of doing things on the line by testing Job's response to suffering.

Frankly, it is surprising that God even entertains a conversation with Satan, but it is even more surprising that God's whole way of operating in the world is on view and on the line. He takes a big risk on Job's reaction to pain.

When you realize that Job doesn't even know what is going on, the risk seems too big. Job doesn't know what has gone on in the heavenly council. He has no idea that God's integrity depends on Job's reaction to what is about to happen. If I were God, I wouldn't risk so much on Job. I think God is majorly unpredictable at this point.

God has sewn unpredictability into creation

The more you get to know God (for example, in the book of Job), the more unpredictability you see. We've already seen that God does not govern our world with a strict law of reward and punishment that says if you suffer, it's because you have sinned. But God has also sewn unpredictability into creation. What do I mean by this? Well, why don't you go to the zoo and look for a long time at a rhinoceros. Just meditate on what an unlikely creature it is. Or have a look at a giraffe. Not even a kid who exercises his wildest imagination could come up with a creature as unpredictable in its design as a giraffe. Have you ever seen the way a giraffe moves? Or watched an elephant and pondered what an unusual thing it is? God has sewn unpredictability into our world. That is what he says in Job 39:

> "The wings of the ostrich flap joyfully,
> > but they cannot compare with the pinions and feathers of the stork.
> She lays her eggs on the ground
> > and lets them warm in the sand,
> unmindful that a foot may crush them,
> > that some wild animal may trample them.
> She treats her young harshly, as if they were not hers,
> > she cares not that her labour was in vain,
> for God did not endow her with wisdom
> > or give her a share of good sense.
> Yet when she spreads her feathers to run,
> > she laughs at horse and rider." (vv. 13-18)

Job demands that God act predictably in his creation—particularly that Job might be shown justice immediately. But God explains that unpredictability is part of the world he created. "Look at the ostrich", he says. "She has fine wings, but she cannot fly. She goes to the trouble of laying her eggs, but she leaves them where other animals can trample them. Not very smart. But boy, can she run! She laughs at the warhorses when she overtakes them." That's why I don't think God is boring: he has sewn unpredictability into the world.

But the thing that really makes me shake my head is that he still entrusts very important things to people like you and me. Not only does he stake his reputation on Job, he has also entrusted sinful people with the job of spreading the good news about Jesus to the ends of the earth. God could have proclaimed it himself from heaven on the first day of every month. He could have written it in the sky. He could have sent out legions of powerful angels to spread the news. He could have created a computer virus that popped up with John 3:16 every time you typed the word 'the'. In fact, God *has* used all of these methods in the past (apart from the computer virus). But instead, he entrusts the future of his kingdom and its message to people like you and me. That's unpredictable; it's not boring.

God does actually care about us

Another reason we get bored with God is that we think that he doesn't really care about all the details of our lives. We think he finds us boring, so we think that if we are uninteresting to him then we might as well be uninterested in him.

My friend Dougal is a teacher at a posh boys' boarding school. The boys don't go home when school is done for the day; they live at school. I think that sounds like a prison, but apparently it costs a lot of money to be a boarder at this school. Usually the boys who are boarders come from way out in the country, so it kind of makes sense for them to live at school. But Dougal told me that some of the boarders come from families who live in the same suburb as the school. Maybe there is a good reason why people who live only a mile from the school might send their son to live there. But, at least in some cases, it seems as though the parents are not interested in their sons—and if that's the case, then it's plain enough to me that those boys will soon lose interest in their parents.

I wonder if we sometimes think that God has just put us here and gotten on with his business, and that could be why we lose interest in God—because we think that we are uninteresting to him.

Appearances can be deceiving

I kind of get why people feel that way, because sometimes God appears to be silent and unavailable. Take the book of Job, for example. There are some 35 chapters of Job—by far and away the majority of the book—where God remains silent. Job complains about this in chapter 23:

> "But if I go to the east, he is not there;
>> if I go to the west, I do not find him.
> When he is at work in the north, I do not see him;
>> when he turns to the south, I catch no glimpse of him." (vv. 8-9)

And later on he says:

> "I cry out to you, O God, but you do not answer;
>> I stand up, but you merely look at me." (Job 30:20)

God seems nowhere to be found, but appearances can often be deceiving. God is at work in the circumstances of our lives, even when he appears to be silent and unavailable. At the big-picture level in Job's life, God has staked his own integrity and reputation on the reaction to suffering of this one man. That means God is pretty interested in the outcome of Job's life. If we zoom in on Job's perspective, we see that God is drawing Job closer to himself, and teaching Job about who he is. God may appear to be silent and unavailable, but that does not make him uninterested.

When God finally breaks his silence in Job 38, that's exactly what he says. God speaks to Job for four whole chapters, and when you first read it, it sounds like Job is getting a lashing from God. But really he is being invited to continue walking with the God who cares about even the details of the lives of the animals. God says:

"Do you hunt the prey for the lioness
    and satisfy the hunger of the lions
when they crouch in their dens
    or lie in wait in a thicket?
Who provides food for the raven
    when its young cry out to God
    and wander about for lack of food?

"Do you know when the mountain goats give birth?
    Do you watch when the doe bears her fawn?
Do you count the months till they bear?
    Do you know the time they give birth?" (Job 38:39-39:2)

Of course Job remains speechless—what answer could he give? Obviously Job doesn't satisfy the hunger of the lions or count down the months until the doe gives birth to her young. The point is that God does. God cares for the animals—even the animals in the wild. God's argument goes like this: "Do you not think, Job, that if I care for the animals then I care for you?" Of course he does.

You need to know that God is interested in you, so that you don't grow bored with him and start your own religion. For your own peace of mind and faith in God, you need to know that he delights in his servants and is interested in their lives enough to make sure that he rights the wrongs done to them.

This is certainly the case for our main man, Job. Remember how proud of Job God is in the opening two chapters of the book? He is like the father of a newborn baby, keen to show him off to anyone who takes an interest.

At the stage of life I am in right now, there are babies everywhere. Everyone is popping them out. My social life is controlled by the needs of infants. I don't go out at night; I go out for brunch. (Who else goes out for brunch? Brunch didn't exist until cafés realized that mid-morning was the only time of the day when people with babies could go out. So they invented a new meal—brunch.) Now, frankly, not all babies are cute; there are some pretty ugly babies. I've seen kids who look more like weasels than babies. Other babies have got heads that are so big and round, they look like bowling balls. I can imagine someone putting two fingers in their eyes and a thumb in their mouth and sending the baby's head down the alley, hoping for a strike. But the thing is that the father is always proud of his little baby, no matter what it looks like. You'd think that if your baby looked like a weasel or a bowling ball, you might be a bit embarrassed or apologetic, but the proud dad is always delighted in his little one.

And that is true here of Job. Of course, Job is not an ugly baby; he is blameless and upright. But to God, he is not just Job; he is servant Job. And not just servant Job, but "*my* servant Job". What a position of honour—to be called a personal servant of the living God! At the beginning of the book, that is exactly what Job is— one in whom God delights. And after the long chapters of silence, and after God questions Job from the storm in the final chapters (Job 38-42), Job is once again "*my* servant Job" (42:7). He is given the honourable task of praying and offering sacrifices for his three friends, with whom God was angry on account of them being useless philosophers and off-the-mark theologians. Job is someone in whom God delights, despite the long silence from God.

I think we all need to hear that, far from finding us uninteresting, God delights in us.

One of the reasons we know that God delights in his people and is interested in them is that he is careful to right the wrongs that happen to them. In the very last part of the book of Job, God rights the wrongs: "the LORD blessed the latter part of Job's life more than the first" (Job 42:12). Job is given twice as many animals as before, and he has more children. His daughters are the most beautiful in the land, and he lives to see his great-grandchildren. He dies "old and full of years" (Job 42:17). That's an old-fashioned way of saying that Job was blessed, which is another way of saying that there was a righting of the wrongs.

Of course, it's worth saying that God may not right *all* the wrongs in this life. If even Jesus—who is described 700 years before his birth as the servant in whom God delights (Isa 42:1)—has to wait until his resurrection for everything to be restored, then we can wait too.

But I really think it is worth knowing that God delights in his servants and rights all wrongs, either now or in the next life. And when you know that, I think you are less tempted to hit the golf course or stay in bed or start your own religion, and more inclined to get to know God better.

God is bigger (and better) than we think

The last thing to realize on this whole topic of evil and suffering is that God is bigger than we think. This means that the Christian life is not about knowing all the answers to life's questions, but about knowing the one who does know all the answers. Sometimes our suffering seems so pointless, and we think that knowing the point of it would make it more bearable. We want answers and we want God to give them to us now.

But we are better off just wanting God. This is the faith journey that Job takes 35 chapters to travel. In chapters 3-37 his friends make accusations about his innocence, much like Satan did in the first two chapters. And Job increasingly seeks an audience with God. He wants his day in court; his questions answered. He even seems pretty flexible about it—at one point he says, "summon me and I will answer, or let me speak, and you reply" (Job 13:22). It's as though he is saying to God, "I can work around you, however you want to play it—let's just talk about it".

We feel that tension in Job's life: we know he is innocent, we know he is suffering, and we want to know when he will get justice. This is the basic question that the to and fro with Job's friends sets up: why does God allow Job to suffer?

How will God answer this question? Like the relief of a late afternoon storm on a stinking hot summer's day, God eventually does break his silence, but he doesn't answer Job's question like we want him to. He doesn't tell us *why* Job has suffered. In fact, he turns the tables on Job and asks dozens of blistering questions from out of a thunderstorm. If ever you doubt the wisdom and power of God, imagine reading those four chapters in one go, outside, at night, in the middle of a thunderstorm. Just a short section will give us the vibe. When God answers Job out of the storm, he says:

> "Who is this that darkens my counsel
>   with words without knowledge?
> Brace yourself like a man;
>   I will question you,
>   and you shall answer me.
>
> "Where were you when I laid the earth's foundation?
>   Tell me, if you understand.

Who marked off its dimensions? Surely you know!
    Who stretched a measuring line across it?
On what were its footings set,
    or who laid its cornerstone …?

"Who shut up the sea behind doors
    when it burst forth from the womb …?

When I said, 'This far you may come and no farther;
    here is where your proud waves halt'?
"Have you ever given orders to the morning,
    or shown the dawn its place …?

"What is the way to the abode of light?
    And where does darkness reside? …

"Can you bind the beautiful Pleiades?
    Can you loose the cords of Orion?
Can you bring forth the constellations in their seasons
    or lead out the Bear with its cubs?
Do you know the laws of the heavens?
    Can you set up God's dominion over the earth?" (Job 38:2-6, 8,
        11-12, 19, 31-33)

Can you imagine being Job at that moment? You are confident of your own integrity and innocence. You rightly want to know why you have suffered unjustly. And then God speaks to you out of a storm, questioning you blisteringly and exhaustively. "I created this universe, not you. I laid out its foundations. I measured it and built it. I shut up the seas and limited them. And I continue to sustain the world. It's me, not you, who brings forth the morning every morning, and brings forth the darkness from its home each night. It is me who controls the movements of the stars. Not you, Job, not you. But me."

Not only does God control the basic elements of the world—earth, sea, sun, stars—but he goes on in those four chapters to show that he made and provides for the untamable animals of the wild—the wild donkey, the wild ox, the ostrich, the horse, the hawk and the eagle. Science can explain *how* the universe works physically, chemically, biologically, whatever. But God can explain the *why*, if he chooses to. God stands behind the order and the design, the seemingly random occurrences and chance events. He even controls the forces of chaos and evil, of death and Satan.[5] Perhaps this explains what we consider to be pointless suffering; it is part of God's bigger work of controlling chaos, evil and Satan.

God breaks his silence with an onslaught of questions … and

yet he doesn't answer Job's question. Frankly, I am surprised that Job is still alive by the end of it. But I reckon the fact that Job is still alive might demonstrate that instead of being a relentless attack from God, Job 38-41 is an invitation to keep trusting God; to keep walking with God and to maintain faith in God, even when you don't have all the answers.

If you didn't have the wisdom to create the universe, then you won't understand everything in it. But that's OK, because you can know the God who *does* understand everything.

If you don't have the power to bring forth the sun each morning, or the stars at night, then you won't know all the mysteries of the cosmos. But that's OK, because you can know the God who *does* know everything.

If you cannot tame the wild animals, let alone provide for them, then you won't understand everything about how God works. But that's OK, because you can know him enough to know him truly.

If you cannot control the forces of chaos and evil, Satan and death, then you cannot know all the answers. But it doesn't matter, because you can know God, who *does* know all the answers.

In April 2006, a goldmine collapsed in Beaconsfield, Tasmania. There were 17 people in the mine at the time; 14 escaped immediately following the collapse and another, Larry Knight, was killed. After five days, two other miners, Todd Russell and Brant Webb, were found alive using a remote control device. It suddenly became an event of national and even international interest. The Foo Fighters even wrote an instrumental song, called 'Ballad of the Beaconsfield Miners', in response. It took a full two weeks to rescue the two miners, who were trapped nearly one kilometre below the surface. The paramedic in charge of getting them out alive, Paul Featherstone, said that the miners would sometimes get frustrated at the long time they had to wait, but that was because they didn't know or understand the very delicate time-consuming operation that was going on above them.

We are often like that when we are wading through suffering. God seems so slow in bringing resolution to difficult situations. Job feels this frustration, but look at what he says when he realizes what is going on above him:

"I know that you can do all things;
  no plan of yours can be thwarted.
You asked, 'Who is this that obscures my counsel without
  knowledge?'
  Surely I spoke of things I did not understand,

> things too wonderful for me to know.
>
> "You said, 'Listen now, and I will speak;
>   I will question you,
>   and you shall answer me.'
> "My ears had heard of you
>   but now my eyes have seen you.
> Therefore I despise myself
>   and repent in dust and ashes." (Job 42:2-6)

Job realizes that his relationship with God is what matters, rather than knowing all the answers. "I spoke of things I did not understand, things too wonderful for me to know ... but I have seen you with my own eyes", he says. What Job had hoped for all that time—that he would see God with his own eyes—has happened. And hearing God is enough for Job; it's more important than having his questions answered. So Job repents, not in the sense that he confesses some non-existent sin (remember, he is presented throughout the book as being upright and righteous), but in the sense that he changes his mind. He no longer wants his day in court, because he has seen God and now realizes how big God is. He has a relationship with God and that is enough for him.

The question is whether it will be enough for us. We need a fair serving of humility to accept that there is something better than knowing all the answers, and that is to know the God who does know all the answers. The Christian life is not based on knowing all the answers, but on a personal relationship with the God who does. He may not speak to you out of a storm. He may not come over for afternoon tea (although he could have if you lived 2,000 years ago in Palestine). But through the death and resurrection of Jesus, it remains possible to have a personal relationship with God. (If you're not a Christian, I strongly encourage you to visit www.twowaystolive.com to find out how and why you can have a personal relationship with God.)

It's plenty OK to search for answers in the middle of tests and trials. But what we really need is a relationship with the living God, the creator and sustainer of the universe, the one who knows and controls everything.

That's where Job arrives at the end of his journey. It is enough for him. Is it enough for you?

Endnotes

1. Michelle Tauber, 'Two Cool', *People Magazine*, vol. 61, no. 17, 3 May 2004, p. 110.
2. See also Luke 13:1-5, where a crowd tells Jesus of a tragedy in which 18 people were killed when the tower of Siloam fell on them. It was a kind of first-century September 11 or Boxing Day tsunami. And Jesus says to them, "Do you think they were more guilty than all the others living in Jerusalem? I tell you, no!" He is saying that the reason the 18 died is not because they were worse sinners than others. But he is also saying that no-one is better off than them, because everyone will follow them into death. Unless we repent, we will die just like they died—only the timing and circumstances of death will be different. We are meant to see our ultimate fate in their deaths and in the deaths of everyone who dies tragically. And we are meant to see the warning that we should repent while we are still alive. In this way, God sovereignly uses the suffering of others for our good—specifically, here, to warn us to repent.
3. CS Lewis, *The Problem of Pain*, HarperCollins, 2001 (1944), p. 91.
4. That's what Sun Myung Moon of Korea did last century. His family was Christian (Presbyterian in fact), but at the age of 16 Moon claims

to have seen a vision of Jesus. In this vision Jesus told him to carry out the task that Jesus himself had failed to complete, because apparently dying on the cross was not part of the plan. Naturally, Sun Myung Moon was the only one who could do it. So he proclaimed himself as the new Messiah and began the Unification Church, nicknamed 'the Moonies'. He is now banned in Britain but has made billions from his followers.

5. The latter part of God's barrage of questions shows that he controls the behemoth and the leviathan, two almost mythical beasts that represent the cosmic forces of chaos and evil, of death and Satan (Job 40:15ff, 41:1ff).

Feedback on this resource

We really appreciate getting feedback about our resources—not just suggestions for how to improve them, but also positive feedback and ways they can be used. We especially love to hear that the resources may have helped someone in their Christian growth.

You can send feedback to us via the 'Feedback' menu in our online store, or write to us at PO Box 225, Kingsford NSW 2032, Australia.

sex

What's the deal with sex anyway? Is it just a physical need that we should satisfy whenever and however we please? Or is it something dirty and sinful that a good Christian should have nothing to do with?

According to Scott Petty, God has a design for sexuality that is much better than both of these options. Scott also deals with some of the common questions young people have about sex:

- How far can I go physically with my girlfriend or boyfriend?
- Is the Bible anti-homosexual?
- What about pornography?

Like all the Little Black Books, this short book is a fun read and gets straight to the point.

FOR MORE INFORMATION OR TO ORDER CONTACT:

Matthias Media	**Matthias Media (USA)**
Telephone: +61-2-9663-1478	Telephone: 1-866-407-4530
Facsimile: +61-2-9663-3265	Facsimile: 724-964-8166
Email: sales@matthiasmedia.com.au	Email: sales@matthiasmedia.com
www.matthiasmedia.com.au	www.matthiasmedia.com

· **Little Black Books** ·
books that get to the point

predestination

Have you ever wondered whether God gave Adam and Eve free will? Or what 'free will' even means?

Have you ever wondered whether God influences us to make the decisions we make day to day? And if he does, how exactly he does it?

Have you ever wanted to know what the Bible means when it says some are chosen or predestined? Is that good news or bad news for us?

If you have been a Christian for any length of time, you have probably wondered about these questions. In this Little Black Book on predestination, Scott Petty brings his trademark humour and clarity to a topic Christians often get tied in knots about.

FOR MORE INFORMATION OR TO ORDER CONTACT:

Matthias Media
Telephone: +61-2-9663-1478
Facsimile: +61-2-9663-3265
Email: sales@matthiasmedia.com.au
www.matthiasmedia.com.au

Matthias Media (USA)
Telephone: 1-866-407-4530
Facsimile: 724-964-8166
Email: sales@matthiasmedia.com
www.matthiasmedia.com

the bible

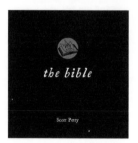

On one hand, millions of people turn to the Bible for guidance of some kind; on the other, just as many dismiss it, mock it, or ignore it. How can a book that is thousands of years old still be relevant today?

Scott Petty writes on what the Bible is and the place it should have in the lives of Christians today, and answers some common questions about the Bible:

- Hasn't science disproved the Bible?
- Doesn't the Bible contradict itself?
- Can I trust the Bible when I'm making decisions?

FOR MORE INFORMATION OR TO ORDER CONTACT:

Matthias Media	**Matthias Media (USA)**
Telephone: +61-2-9663-1478	Telephone: 1-866-407-4530
Facsimile: +61-2-9663-3265	Facsimile: 724-964-8166
Email: sales@matthiasmedia.com.au	Email: sales@matthiasmedia.com
www.matthiasmedia.com.au	www.matthiasmedia.com

If I were God, I'd end all the Pain

A child catches a rare brain virus and is affected for life. A father dies in a plane crash. A dictator murders millions.

Why doesn't God do something about things like this? Why does he allow them to happen? In fact, can we still believe in God in the face of all the suffering and pain in the world?

In this short book, John Dickson looks honestly at these questions and provides some compelling answers. He looks briefly at the alternative explanations for suffering provided by Hinduism, Buddhism, Islam and Atheism, before turning to what the Bible itself says about God, justice and suffering.

FOR MORE INFORMATION OR TO ORDER CONTACT:

Matthias Media	**Matthias Media (USA)**
Telephone: +61-2-9663-1478	Telephone: 1-866-407-4530
Facsimile: +61-2-9663-3265	Facsimile: 724-964-8166
Email: sales@matthiasmedia.com.au	Email: sales@matthiasmedia.com
www.matthiasmedia.com.au	www.matthiasmedia.com

Hanging in There

Hanging in There is a book about God, you, the Bible, prayer, church, relationships, sex, feelings, doubts, love and, above all, hanging in there as a Christian. If you're a young Christian (teenager to early 20s), new to the Christian faith or a long-serving Christian who could use some encouragement, this book is for you.

FOR MORE INFORMATION OR TO ORDER CONTACT:

Matthias Media	**Matthias Media (USA)**
Telephone: +61-2-9663-1478	Telephone: 1-866-407-4530
Facsimile: +61-2-9663-3265	Facsimile: 724-964-8166
Email: sales@matthiasmedia.com.au	Email: sales@matthiasmedia.com
www.matthiasmedia.com.au	www.matthiasmedia.com